GEOGRAPHY 2
LANDFORMS AND FEATURES

GEOGRAPHY FOR KIDS
PLATEAUS, PENINSULAS, DELTAS AND MORE

4th Grade Children's Science Education Books

BABY PROFESSOR
EDUCATION KIDS

Speedy Publishing LLC

40 E. Main St. #1156

Newark, DE 19711

www.speedypublishing.com

Copyright 2017

In this book, we're going to talk about the different types of landforms on Earth. So, let's get right to it!

WHAT IS A LANDFORM?

A landform is a natural, physical feature of Earth's surface. Some of the major landforms are mountains and plains. However, landforms aren't always land. An ocean is a landform because it was formed naturally and covers part of the Earth's surface.

Volcano

Desert

Mountains

Hills
Island
Canyon
Ocean
River
Jungle
Marshes
Waterfall
Plain
DIFFERENT LANDFORMS

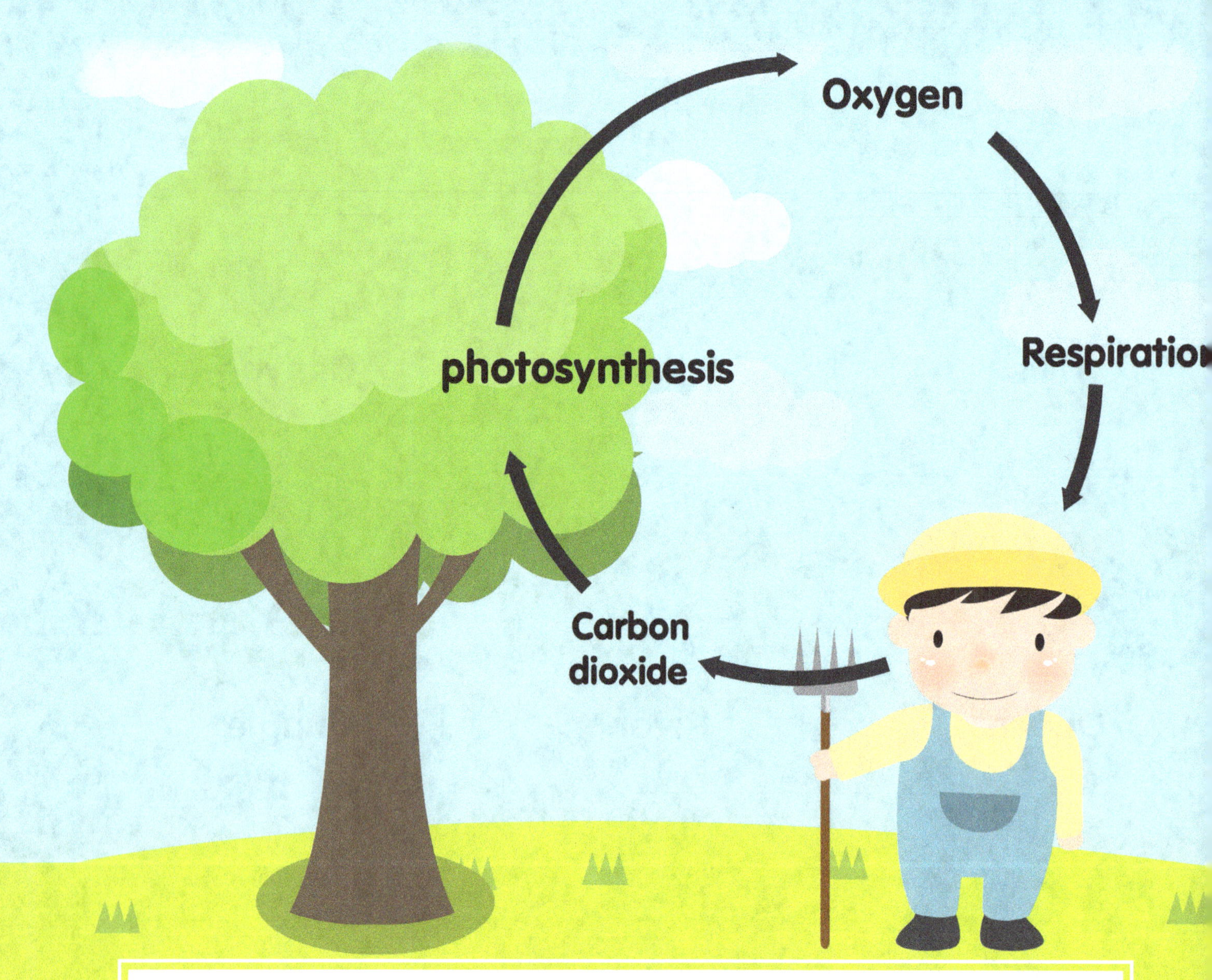

However, oxygen from the atmosphere wouldn't be considered a landform, because it isn't part of the Earth's surface.

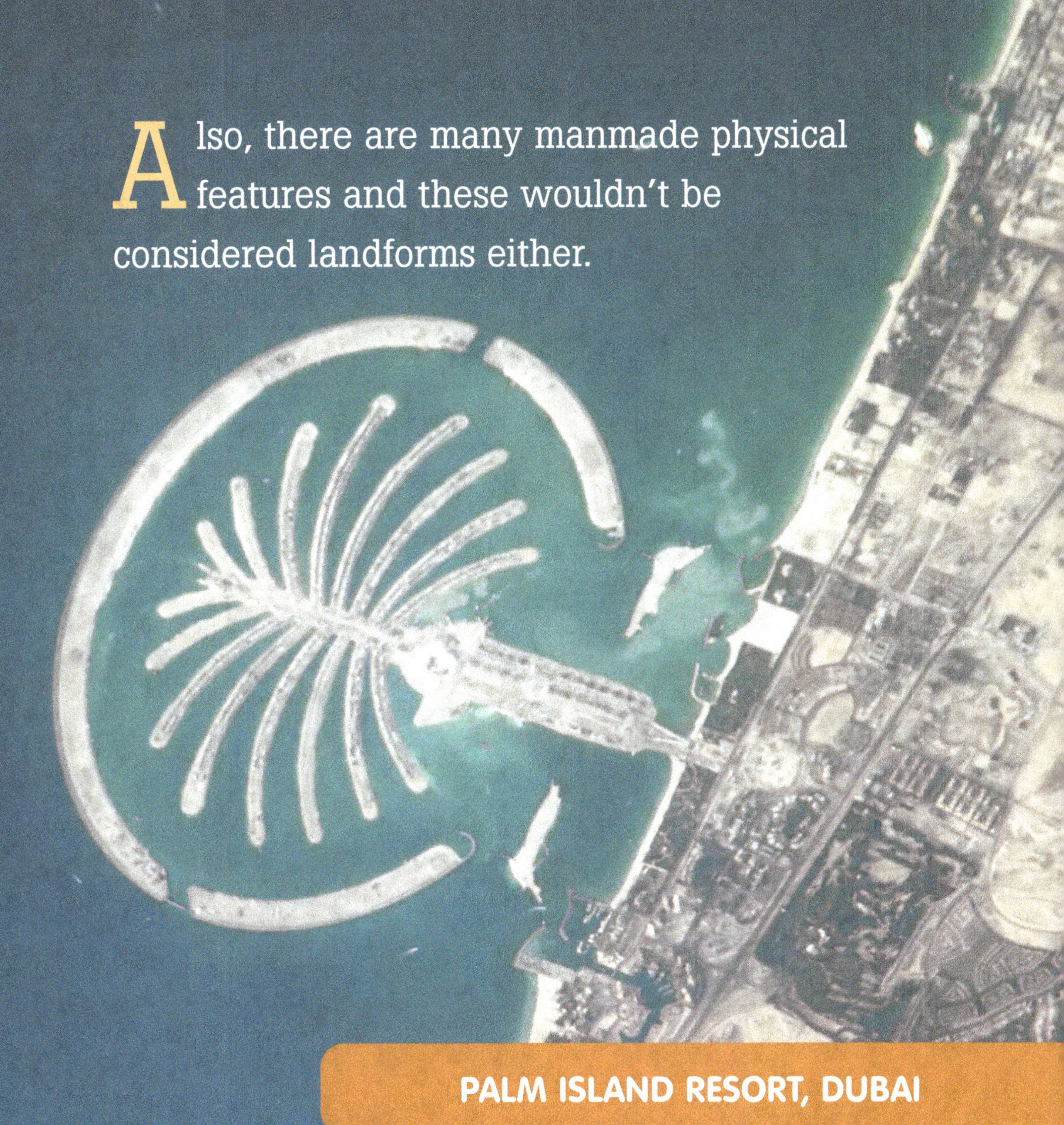

Also, there are many manmade physical features and these wouldn't be considered landforms either.
PALM ISLAND RESORT, DUBAI

Rübezahlwanderweg 60 min

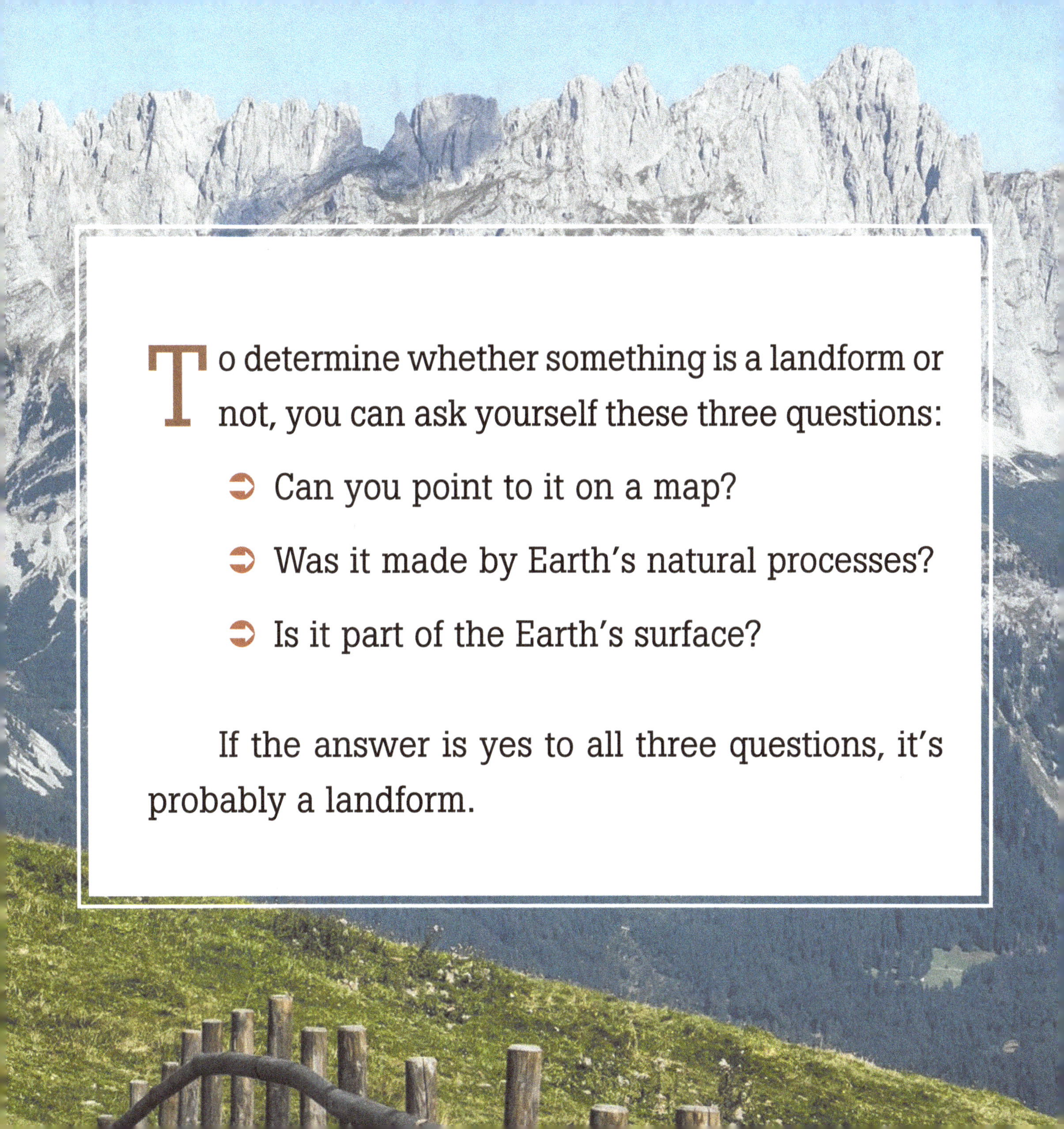

To determine whether something is a landform or not, you can ask yourself these three questions:

- Can you point to it on a map?

- Was it made by Earth's natural processes?

- Is it part of the Earth's surface?

If the answer is yes to all three questions, it's probably a landform.

HOW ARE LANDFORMS CREATED?

Some landforms are created over millions of years while others might be created in just a few hours. The forces of wind and water create landforms. The movements of tectonic plates and volcanic activity are other powerful forces that shape the Earth's surface. Ice from glaciers shapes landforms as well.

FOUR IMPORTANT CHARACTERISTICS OF LANDFORMS

Geologists study landforms. They research these four characteristics:

- Structure, which is the materials the landform is made of and how those materials are arranged

- Process, which is the combination of forces that created the landform, such as wind, pressure, or ice

- Slope, which is the landform's steepness and gives geologists clues concerning how it was formed and its structure

➲ Drainage, which is basically the speed that water drains away from the landform and has an impact on its shape and how it evolves into another form, such as a plateau that becomes a mesa

TYPES OF LANDFORMS

There are many different types of landforms. Here are some of the major types.

MOUNTAINS

If a landform is taller than the areas around it, it may be a mountain. Mountains are the tallest landforms on Earth's surface. A series of mountains is called a range of mountains.

Although there isn't an official definition for how high a mountain must be, most mountains have a height of 1000 feet or more.

MOUNT CLEVELAND VOLCANO
ISLANDS OF FOUR MOUNTAINS

Mountains generally are rather cone-like in shape. They have sides that are steep and pointed tops called peaks.

There are three main types of mountains:

Volcanic

Volcanic mountains are created when molten rock erupts from the inside of the Earth and pours out as lava. When the lava cools it forms new solid rock.

Fold

Fold mountains are created when one tectonic plate pushes against another. The location where they collide with one another is described as the convergent plate boundary.

Block

Block mountains form when there are cracks in the Earth's crust, called faults. Some blocks are forced up and some are forced down. Instead of folding over as with fold mountains, the layers of rock break up into blocks.

Hills

Hills are generally lower than the landforms described as mountains, although there is not a set height for a mountain versus a hill. Just like there are ranges of mountains, there can also be a group of hills that is described as a range. Because they're not usually as tall as mountains, hills have a fairly pleasant climate compared to mountain peaks, which can get very cold due to their elevations.

CHOCOLATE HILLS, BOHOL, PHILIPPINES

STEHEKIN RIVER VALLEY

VALLEYS

Valleys are low-lying landforms that are between two mountainous or hilly regions. As water flows down the steep sides of mountains or hills, it erodes the rocks and topsoil. Over a long period of time, it carves out grooves that are shaped like the letter "V." As the grooves get both wider and deeper, the low-lying land becomes a valley. If a valley is very narrow in width, it's called a canyon.

Another way that valleys can be formed is by very large, slow-moving glaciers. These types of valleys are created when glaciers travel both across and then down a steep slope. This type of action, as a glacier carves out a "U-shaped" valley, is described as scouring.

M any ancient civilizations, such as the Indus
Valley civilization, began in valleys. Most
valleys have pleasant climates, fertile land, and
abundant sources of water.

PLATEAUS

A plateau is a highland region with a top that is flat and sides that are steep. It's sometimes called a tableland due to its shape. The steep faces of rock on all sides of a plateau are called cliffs.

These landforms are created when very hot magma rises toward the Earth's surface from under its crust. In this case, the magma doesn't break through but instead it causes the crust to become elevated forming a plateau.

MESA

Mesas begin as flat plains, but waterways such as rivers and streams erode away some of the land and what is left is a mountain with a flat top. Many geologists feel that a mesa must have some kind of water source. Cattle could graze on top of a mesa but not on top of a butte.

ENCHANTED MESA

WEST MITTEN BUTTE IN
MONUMENT VALLEY

BUTTE

Buttes are smaller than plateaus or mesas. A butte is a small mountain that has a flat top. So, in order from smallest to largest these landforms would be: butte, mesa, and plateau.

PLAINS

Expansive areas of flat land are called plains. Sometimes plains meet at the edges of oceans or seas. These types of plains are called coastal plains. Some plains are formed by the flow of rivers. River plains generally have fertile soil that's good for crops. Many plains are heavily populated because they are easy places to build.

DESERTS

There are two types of deserts. There are hot deserts, such as the Sahara Desert, and there are cold deserts, such as the Arctic desert. Deserts are areas that get very little rainfall throughout the year. They have small amounts of vegetation if they have any at all.

Hot deserts are generally covered in sand and cold deserts are generally covered in ice or snow. The Gobi desert, which is located in Asia, is an exception.

It's rocky but due to its elevation it's also very cold. All deserts have extreme weather conditions. In some deserts, the daytime is intensely hot, but the night is freezing cold.

DUNES

Dunes are sand mounds that are formed by the wind. They happen frequently in deserts and also along the coasts of bodies of water.

ISLANDS

Islands are composed of land that has water on all sides. Islands are formed when volcanoes erupt or when hot spots occur in the Earth's crust and upper mantle, which is called the lithosphere.

CAPE

A cape is a high elevation of land that juts out into a waterway, such as a lake or ocean. For example, Cape Cod juts out into the Atlantic Ocean like a bent arm.

DELTAS

A delta is a piece of land where a river empties into another waterway. For example, the delta of the Nile River empties into the Mediterranean Sea. Deltas are composed of sand and other particles of rock that accumulate into a triangular area.

BAKER RIVER DELTA

NORTH FORK OF THE SMITH RIVER

RIVERS

Rivers are composed of flowing water. They channel into larger bodies of waters such as lakes, seas, or oceans.

ISTHMUS

An isthmus is a very narrow piece of land that connects two large landmasses. The Isthmus of Panama is an example. It connects North America to South America.

CORINTH ISTHMUS

OCEANS

Oceans are the largest bodies of salt water on the Earth. The oceans were formed by the movement of the tectonic plates on Earth's surface. Oceans cover more than 71% of the Earth's surface and because of this they are very important to both the Earth's climate and weather. There are five oceans on Earth but they are all interconnected and can be thought of as one large ocean.

GLACIERS

Glaciers are formed by layers of snow that become compressed to form enormous bodies of ice. Pressure and gravity are the factors that cause them to move.

Alpine glaciers form in high mountainous areas and continental glaciers form in the regions close to the poles.

FLORIDA AERIAL VIEW

PENINSULAS

Peninsulas are pieces of land that are surrounded by water on three of their sides and connected to land on one side. For example, the state of Florida is a peninsula.

SUMMARY

The Earth's surface has many different kinds of physical features. These landforms sometimes happen quickly and sometimes they take millions of years. For example, sand dunes happen quickly, but canyons are formed over millions of years. Landforms are made by nature, not by man. Wind, water, and volcanic activity shape the Earth. All landforms are part of the Earth's surface and they can be located on maps. Landforms don't have to be land. They can also be natural bodies of water.

Awesome! Now that you've read about the different landforms on Earth you may want to read more about the geography of the Northeast States in the Baby Professor book Geography of the US – Northeast States – New York, New Jersey, Maine, Massachusetts and More) | Geography for Kids – US States.

Visit

www.BabyProfessorBooks.com

to download Free Baby Professor eBooks
and view our catalog of new and exciting
Children's Books